It's Up to Me

MINISTRY ACTIVITIES *for* OLDER CHILDREN

Kathy Sapp Osenberger

New Hope
Birmingham, Alabama

New Hope
P. O. Box 12065
Birmingham, AL 35202-2065

©1997 by New Hope
All rights reserved. First printing 1997
Printed in the United States of America

Dewey Decimal Classification: C226.4
Subject Headings: BIBLE—NEW TESTAMENT—LUKE
                      CHRISTIAN LIFE—CHILDREN

Cover design by Mark Smothers

ISBN: 1-56309-206-9
N977103•0597•5M1

"IT'S UP TO ME"

What does that mean?

Have you ever thought of Bible stories as guidelines for daily living? Did you know that the things Jesus did and the stories He told were meant to teach you something TODAY? As you read stories in the New Testament about Jesus, you will see that Jesus wants you to follow His example of caring for others.

In the pages of this book you will find stories, questions to think about (*What Does This Mean to Me?*) and ideas for ways you can care for others (*It's Up to Me*). The stories may be written a little differently, but they are familiar stories from the New Testament book of Luke. Sometimes you may just want to read and think about the story. Maybe it will remind you of a friend or a prayer need.

Sometimes you may want to do the activities. These are just ideas. You may think of other ways to do something for someone else. As you make your way through this book, you will likely discover many new ways of caring for others that you haven't thought of before. You may decide to take on the challenge of living by Jesus' example every day! But remember—it's up to you!

Come See Jesus

You should have been with us. We just marched right up the stairs and started tearing away the roof. We lowered Companius right down to Jesus' feet, and Jesus healed him. It was wonderful.

I want to tell everyone the good news. Sometimes, I get a little ahead of myself. Please forgive me. Let me introduce myself. My name is Palius. I live in one of the towns near the Lake of Gennesaret. My friends and I had been hearing about a man named Jesus who healed people. Our friend, Companius, has been crippled for many years. He had never been able to stand up or walk around. The more that we heard about Jesus, we just knew that Jesus could help Companius.

We found the house where Jesus was teaching that day. Three of my friends and I each took a corner of his mat and carried Companius to the house. We went to the front door first. We hoped that there would be a line to see Jesus, but there was not. People kept coming to see Jesus, and no one stayed in any order. Young men, older women, young women with children, and older men all heard about Jesus and crowded into the doors of the house. Rows and rows of people stood outside the house all trying to hear and see Jesus. People were sitting in the windows of the house, too.

We listened for almost an hour, but it was very hard to hear what Jesus was saying. No one would move aside for us to get in to see Jesus. We were ready to give up and go back home.

As we talked together, Jonas came up with an idea. At first we weren't sure if it would work, but we decided to try. We just had to get Companius in to see Jesus. We knew that Jesus could help Companius like He had helped the leper (see Luke 17:11–19).

The house was just like all the others here in Palestine. The roof was flat, with just a slight slant for the rain water to run off. It was so easy for us to remove some tiles and clear out a space. (This family had a strong roof—it was deep and filled with straw to protect the family from the hot sun.) We then found some ropes, tied the ropes to the corners of Companius's mat and lowered him down to Jesus.

You should have seen the faces of the people sitting near Jesus! Some were still brushing dust and pieces of tile off their clothes. Many mouths were open in amazement at Companius coming down from the roof.

We lowered Companius and his mat right down to Jesus' feet. And guess what Jesus said! He said, "Companius, your sins are forgiven." When some of the religious leaders heard this, they began talking to each other. They thought Jesus was lying. They said to themselves, "Only God can forgive sins. Jesus should ask forgiveness for pretending to be God!"

Well, Jesus was smarter than all of them. He knew what they were thinking and saying. He even asked them, "Why do you think such things?" Then to prove to them that He had the authority to forgive sins, he told Companius, "Get up! Pick up your mat and walk home."

Companius stood up and rolled up his mat. Companius stood up! I had never seen Companius standing or walking. This was a miracle from God.

Companius was so thankful that Jesus had healed him. Immediately he began praising God. We ran down the roof steps and met Companius outside of the house. As we walked home, we sang songs of praise and prayed prayers of thanks to God.

You know, we took the time to help a friend that day. But we were the ones who came away praising God. Amazing! I'm glad that Jonas said, "Come and go with me to see Jesus."

(based on Luke 5:17–26)

What Does This Mean to Me?

Jesus welcomed these men who brought their friend to be healed. Just as Palius cared enough to take his friend to Jesus, you can help your friends know about Jesus and who He is. Fill in answers to the following statements and questions.

Describe a friend. _____

_____

_____

_____

How would you like a friend to help you? _____

_____

How do you help a friend? _____

_____

_____

How could you help a friend know about Jesus?
Here are some suggestions:
- be kind
- share extra magazines from church or a Bible
- invite to church
- talk about what you learn at church

Do you have any more ideas? Write them here.

_____

_____

_____

JOURNAL

Begin a journal. A journal may be 10–12 pages of
notebook paper stapled together or tied with string.
A journal may be a file on your computer or word
processor. For your first entry in your journal, write a
prayer about friendship. Share your prayer with one
friend.

It's Up to Me

Think about what you learned from this story about Jesus.

Make a card for a friend. Thank him or her for his or her friendship. Include your favorite Scripture passage in your card. Choose a time to surprise your friend with the card.

Ask a friend to help as you help someone else. Some suggestions are:
- Mow or rake the yard for someone who is elderly. (Don't let the yard-owner pay you for your time.)
- Run errands for someone who has broken an arm, leg, or hip.
- Spend a few hours playing with a smaller child.
- Read to the child or play games outside with the child to help the parent or grandparent.

Invite someone who doesn't usually go to church to go with you to an activity at church. This friend might be someone who lives in your neighborhood or someone who is in your class at school.

A Changed Life

"Hi, Zacch. It's good to see you today." said Jacob.

"Hey, Zacch. How's business?" said Saul, as he and Jacob passed Zacchaeus on the busy main street in Jericho.

"Hi guys. It's great to see you. Business is fine." replied Zacchaeus as he continued walking toward his office.

I joined Zacch in the cool shade of his inner office. We settled into a relaxed conversation.

"Zacch, the whole business community is curious. Everyone is talking about the change in you. You came back to all your employees and repaid each of them a tremendous amount of money. You are a new person. Tell me about it."

"Matthew, you are a former tax collector. You know the terrible hatred the Jewish people have for tax collectors. I am the chief tax collector for this area of the city. I have many collectors under me," explained Zacchaeus. "I used to demand my share of the taxes plus the amount required by the Roman government. I knew that each of my collectors added their own fees to the amount of money each family paid as taxes.

"I was a wealthy man." Zacchaeus continued. "I could go anywhere I wanted, buy anything that I could see. The Roman officials were pleased with my work. I had political power. But no one here in Jericho had time for me. I was never included in polite conversations. I tried going to the Temple for a while, but I never felt welcome there. I was an outcast.

"For a long time I heard the name Jesus. One day I overheard someone telling about Jesus' sermons. Another day I heard someone tell of their cousin who had been healed by Jesus. The name Jesus kept coming up in conversations around me. I'll admit, I was really curious about this Jesus. Then, I heard that Jesus was coming to Jericho. People all over the city were talking about it.

"I thought, well, now's my chance to see this Jesus everyone has been talking about. Since I have such an important community position, surely Jesus will see me," said Zacchaeus.

"So I walked out to the road where Jesus was rumored to be passing through town. Matthew, you should have seen the crowd. There were people everywhere," related Zacchaeus.

Matthew chuckled, "Yes Zacch, I remember, I was with Jesus on that day. I was inside the crowd that was walking with Jesus."

"Oh yes, that's right. Well, you know that the crowds were huge—rows and rows of people. As I neared the crowd, my heart fell. How was I going to see Jesus? I am so short. I never see well in crowds. I knew that the people were not going to let me in the front to see Jesus. Then, I saw a beautiful tall sycamore tree. That was it. The sycamore tree was my answer," described Zacchaeus. "The last time I climbed a tree I was just a boy, but I still remem-bered how to climb one. Right there on the main road in Jericho, I climbed that tree. I had to see Jesus.

"Sitting in the tree I waited and watched for Jesus. But, Matthew, you know what happened next?" said Zacchaeus.

"Yes, that's right. I was there watching Jesus visit with the crowds. Jesus had such a way with people. Jesus took time with many people that day. And then, Jesus stopped in front of your sycamore tree. I thought Jesus was stopping in the shade to rest. We had been traveling all day. But, Jesus looked up and called you by name. I thought you were going to fall out of the tree," Matthew chuckled.

"Yes, I was a bit startled when Jesus called me by name. I think all the good Jewish citizens around me were a bit surprised, too. Jesus was actually talking to a tax collector. What gossip that caused! And then, Jesus asked to come to my home. I felt such a warmth, such acceptance, such love from Jesus. I knew I had not been honest in my business dealings. Jesus knew also, but He still loved me and wanted to have a meal with me—a tax collector!" said Zacchaeus.

"After the day with Jesus, I knew I must make my business dealings more honest. I gave half of my possessions to the poor. Plus I went back through my account books. If I had cheated any family out of money, I returned four dollars for every one dollar that I cheated the family. The staff in my office was amazed. They were a tremendous help in returning the money. I don't miss the things that I gave away. Jesus came into my life and changed me. I am truly a changed person. I have a new life," concluded Zacchaeus.

"We have certainly seen a change in you, Zacch. Jesus seems to know the people who are difficult to love in the world, and He shows that He loves them. I hope that we can continue to show Jesus' love to others. Thanks for the visit, Zacch," said Matthew.

"Thank you for coming. Hope to see you again soon. My greetings to Jesus and the other disciples. Good-bye," answered Zacchaeus.

(based on Luke 19:1–10)

What Does This Mean to Me?

Think about the answers to these questions and write them below.

Do you know a person at school who is hard to like? In the neighborhood? At church? _____

_____

_____

_____

Why is this person hard for you to like? _____

_____

_____

How might this person feel about being left out of

activities or being picked last for teams?_____

_____

_____

Are there ways that you can be nice to a person who is hard to like? _____

_____

_____

_____

Could you:
- Talk to the person?
- Invite this person to your home for a meal or after school snack?
- Give the person a real compliment?
- Invite this person to go to a movie? or to church?

List here other ways you can be nice to someone.

_____

_____

_____

JOURNAL

In your journal, write your thoughts about a person who is difficult to like. Read your thoughts aloud to God. Wait for a few minutes, then continue to write your thoughts, if you have any others.

It's Up to Me

With an adult's help, find clothes in your closet that are too small for you. Give these clothes to a crisis center or clothing closet. Ask for a tour of the crisis center or clothing closet. Ask about ways that you could help at the center once a month.

Say something nice to every person that you meet today. Be sincere. People will know when the compliments are not honest.

Some ideas are:
- As you pass the neighbors down the street, tell them how nice their garden looks.
- Tell someone at school that you like the color of their backpack.
- Compliment your dad on how shiny his shoes look this morning.
- Thank your mom or dad for preparing dinner for the family.

S T O R Y

Different Ways to Serve

I love those two sisters of mine! We are very close for a brother and two sisters. But they are sometimes as different as night and day. Let's see. . . how can I describe them?

Martha always has a list of things to do. Because of her, our home is always spotless. Martha gets up early in the morning, spends time in prayer and is busy about her tasks. Martha is a marvelous cook. I've gained some weight since I have been living with her. If a new person in town needs a meal or a place to stay overnight, Martha volunteers. People like to come to our home because Martha knows how to make our guests feel welcome.

Martha has a busy schedule because she does a lot to help people in our community. I sometimes have a hard time keeping up with all she is doing.

And Mary . . . Mary keeps busy, too. But Mary spends time thinking as she works. Mary listens to others and shows her love for others by listening. She likes to learn, especially about God. Mary is usually quiet when we have a group of people in our home. She enjoys having guests in our home, but she likes to quietly move from person to person talking to each one. Mary spends lots of her time with others. When someone has a need, Mary is very generous with all she has.

I remember a time when I saw how different my sisters are. Knowing He was always welcome, Jesus came to our home on His way to Jerusalem. Even though He seemed very tired from His trip, Jesus

12

insisted on talking with Martha, Mary, and me. We talked all afternoon and into the evening. Jesus and the disciples had been going from village to village, healing the sick, casting out demons, and teaching about the love of God. As always, Jesus' visits became times for us to learn from Him about God.

Mary had greeted Jesus with a basin to wash His feet and sat down to listen. Martha wanted to hear Jesus' stories, too, but she quietly went to the kitchen and began to prepare the evening meal. So Mary sat listening to Jesus while Martha prepared dinner.

I could hear Martha banging pots and pans as she put them into the oven. Finally, Martha came back into where Mary and I were talking to Jesus. Martha asked loudly, "Jesus, don't You care that my sister has left all the work for me to do? Tell her to come and help me."

I'll never forget the kind, caring look on Jesus face when He said, "Martha, Martha! You are worried over many things—many dishes of food, but just one dish is needed. Come and spend time with Me tonight. Mary has chosen to spend time with Me. Spending time together is what is most important to Me right now. Please don't take this away from her or from Me."

Jesus' words were hard for Martha to hear, but I needed to be reminded of them as well. Spending time with Jesus is just as important as doing things to help others.

My sisters are both great women. Each one, in all that she does, serves Jesus in her own way. Each one shows she loves Jesus in her own way. Sometimes Jesus needs someone to cook and clean for Him. Sometimes Jesus needs someone to sit and be with Him. I am thankful that we can be a home where we all love Jesus, each in his or her own way.

(based on Luke 10:38–42)

What Does This Mean to Me?
Think about and answer the following questions.

What are some things that you do very well? _____

_____

_____

_____

_____

_____

What are some things that your sister, brother, or
friend does very well? _____

_____

_____

_____

_____

_____

What things on your lists are the same? _____

_____

_____

_____

_____

What things on your lists are different? _____

_____

_____

_____

_____

_____

JOURNAL

Show someone else these questions. Ask him or her
to answer the questions. Compare your answers. Talk
to that person about the ways you use your talents
to help others. Write in your journal about your talents. Write a prayer of thanksgiving to God for your
talents.

It's Up to Me

Choose one or two storybooks written for younger children. Using a cassette tape recorder, read the books aloud and record them. You may also want to tell a Bible story on the tape. Ask your parent or a leader at church to help you contact a day care center or children's hospital. Mail or take the tape to the center or hospital for children who cannot read or don't feel like reading. Pray for the children who will listen to your tape.

Collect magazines and other Christian literature to place in a coin laundry, doctor's office, and other waiting areas. Affix stickers with a Bible verse or encouraging message. Ask your brother, sister, or good friend to help you deliver these. Make sure you have permission from the owners to leave the literature in these places.

Watch for ways to keep your community beautiful. Look at a park, a vacant area in your neighborhood, or the side of your street. Invite your family to help you clean the area, gathering trash into garbage cans or bags. Report anything unsafe to an adult.

S T O R Y

4

Letter to the Editor
JERUSALEM TIMES, EVENING EDITION

Dear Editor,

Last week I was traveling from your fine city after conducting my business. I exited the city on the Jericho Road. I knew traveling alone could be dangerous, but I had further business appointments in Jericho and needed to hurry. So I set out on my journey.

Only a mile or so on my journey, the road narrowed and became full of rocks. The twists and turns in the road were quick and steep. In the heat of the day, I questioned my decision to travel this road that was surrounded by desert on all sides. I must tell you that I was feeling very alone.

I walked a few more minutes and decided that the road downhill to Jericho would be easier to continue than to turn back and return uphill to Jerusalem. Feeling a little more positive, I continued my journey.

Then a dreadful thing happened. Several men came from behind the rocks. One hit me in the face. Another man pushed me into a rock. As I fell to the ground, I felt another kick me in the stomach. I tried to stand, but I could not. I was bleeding, and my entire body hurt. The men took my valuables and ran off into the desert. I had no strength to chase after the thieves. I could only lie on the ground and hold my stomach.

17

It felt like I had been lying on the ground for a long time before someone passed. I called out as best I could, but I guess the person couldn't hear me. After another long wait, I heard the rustle of clothing and the flip, flop of a person's sandals. Someone else was coming. I gathered all the strength that I could and called out to this person. I heard the person walk a little slower, but that person didn't stop either.

The sun was beginning to fall in the sky, so I could tell that the afternoon was nearing evening. So I waited and waited.

I must have fallen asleep for a time. I was startled to hear and feel someone near me. Someone had stopped to help—without thought for his own safety. I had no strength to speak; the only sound out of my mouth was a moan of pain. The person spoke quietly and calmly. I don't remember the person's words, but I do remember his gentle touch as he cleaned my wounds. The softness of cloth was all I felt as he applied to my cuts.

The person who stopped helped me up from the ground and onto his animal. I don't remember how long we traveled, but soon I was lifted off the animal and carried indoors.

I slept most of the night and next morning. When I awoke, the gentle caregiver was gone. The innkeeper told me my bill was paid and I had several days to heal before I continued my business and joined a caravan to go home.

The other travelers who passed by me may have been busy and unable to stop due to important meetings. Some people may have felt I deserved my injury because I decided to travel alone. The other travelers may not have had any first aid supplies with them. They may have gone into the city to get supplies or to send someone to get me. I really don't know why the others did not stop.

This letter is to express my thanks for the courageous person who cared generously for me in my time of need. I was sick and was comforted. At a time of great need I was given help. This person gave willingly of his time and money to care for me as I recovered from a violent attack and theft. This experience gives me hope that there are people who care—even for foolish travelers like me. I am very grateful.

Sincerely,
T. R. Aveler

(based on Luke 10:29–37)

What Does This Mean to Me?

Think about the answers to these questions and statements and write them below.

Name some ways that you helped someone this week.

_____

_____

_____

Why did you help that person? _____

_____

_____

_____

How did you feel after you helped him or her?_____

_____

_____

_____

_____

Would you help someone again? Why or why not?

_____

_____

_____

_____

JOURNAL

In your journal, keep a list of ways people help other people. Write this list for a week (or two). In your journal, tell about how the person helping might feel. Also tell how the person being helped might feel. Write a prayer thanking God for people who are loving as they help others.

It's Up to Me

Make a "Use Me" book.
Supplies: 6-7 pieces of white paper, 2 pieces of construction paper, thin markers, 3-4 new crayons, a new pencil or pen, one stick of gum, one piece of individually wrapped candy, one letter envelope and postage stamp, stapler, clear plastic tape

With the thin markers, write on one page, "Chew Me." Then attach the stick of gum to the paper. On a second page use the plastic tape to attach the new crayons and write "Color Me." For this page you might use a clean page from a coloring book. Write, "Enjoy Me," on a third page and attach the piece of candy. On the next page write about yourself. Use the title "Meet Me" for this page. Fold one piece of paper and place it in the envelope. Write your address on the envelope. Attach the envelope to another page of plain paper and write, "Write Me," on this page. When all your pages are complete, make a cover for your book with the construction paper pieces. Staple all the pages together. Write on your front cover, "Use Me." Give this book to a local clothing closet or crisis shelter.

Purchase or make a teddy bear for your police department. Police officers use these toys to give to children who are in automobile accidents. Invite someone from the police department to tell a group at church about the teddy bears and how they are used.

Words for Neighbors

Fill in the blanks for these verses about neighbors.

"L__v__ th__ n__ __ ghb__r __s th__s__lf"
(Galatians 5:14b KJV).

"D__n't pl__n __nyth__ng th__t w__ll h__rt
y__ __ r n__ __ghb__r; h__ l__v__s b__s__d__
y__ __, tr__st__ng y__ __"
(Proverbs 3:29 CEV).

"L__v__ w__rk__th n__ __ll t__ h__s
n__ __ghb__r"
(Romans 13:10a KJV).

"Sp__ __k __v__ry m__n tr__th w__th h__s
n__ __ghb__r"
(Ephesians 4:25b KJV).

Can you find other verses about neighbors in the
Bible? List what you find below. _____

_____

_____

_____

_____

Praying or Bragging?

The Pharisee comes into the Temple walking confidently to his usual place to sit and pray—right in the center of the courtyard. The Pharisee is a tall man. People look up to him as they come into the Temple courtyard to pray. The Pharisee looks around at the people as they look at him. Actually, he looks out above the crowd and prays like this:

Dear Holy, Righteous, and Almighty God,
I come to you at this holy hour—the fourth prayer time of each day—just as I always come to pray, every day. As I came into the Temple today, I came to my usual pew. People scooted down when I came up. They knew that I would want my usual place to pray.

As I came in to pray today, I recognized so many people. The people were people that I knew were unfair in their business practices; some had cheated their customers. I would never cheat my customers as much as they do. I even saw someone who bragged about being dishonest on his taxes. I would never be dishonest on my taxes.

God, You know that I fast twice a week. Twice is more than the biblical law requires. And when the offering plate is passed, I always give the Temple a tenth of all money that I receive. A tenth is so easy to figure, and I am very good at math. I check my math and make sure I am giving a tenth—no more and no less.

I don't have anything more to pray about until next prayer time. **Amen.**

Satisfied with his prayer, the Pharisee walks out of the courtyard, congratulating himself on completing another day's prayer obligations.

❖ ❖ ❖ ❖ ❖ ❖ ❖ ❖ ❖ ❖ ❖

Hesitating a little, the Tax Collector walks quietly into the Temple courtyard. His steps are heavy and slow. It has been a long time between his visits to the Temple for prayer. But this time the Tax Collector comes with a purpose, too. His emotion swells with each step he takes into the courtyard. The Tax Collector feels the tears begin to run down his cheek. The Tax Collector is very aware of his own sins. He knows that he has been greedy. He knows that he has not been totally honest in his business dealings with others.

That's why the Tax Collector is looking at the floor. He bows his head low. He can only find a cold Temple column to lean on. The column is a good place to hide—or to try to hide from God. Tears form a puddle on the floor in front of the Tax Collector as he prays like this:

Dear God,
I am a sinner. I have too many sins to name. I am sorry. Please forgive me. I know that I deserve much punishment for my sins. Please be merciful to me. **Amen.**

(based on Luke 18:9–14)

What Does This Mean to Me?

Jesus told this story to illustrate how important it is for you to be sincere when you pray. Of these two men, which one do you think was more sincere? Which one was praying, and which one was bragging? By telling this story, Jesus explained how God appreciates and listens to those who are humble when they pray.

Think about the answers to these questions and write them below.

What does it mean to brag? _____

_____

_____

_____

Do people brag in their prayers?

    Yes   No

How should you pray? _____

_____

_____

_____

Luke 18:13b (NIV) says, "'God, have mercy on me, a sinner.'" What is mercy? _____

_____

_____

_____

JOURNAL

What are some other words that can be used for mercy? _____ _____ _____ _____

Pray for God's help as you plan to go through one or two hours—or a whole day—not talking about yourself. Listen to others. Write in your journal how you felt at the end of the time. Include a prayer of thanksgiving for the people you listened to today. Ask God to help you to be a better listener at school, at home, and when you are with friends.

It's Up to Me

Look for a person at school from a different language or ethnic background. This person may be new to your school or may be new in your neighborhood. This person may be trying to learn English. Pray for this person daily for a week. Then ask this person to teach you some of their language. Work on a project together—making a model airplane or baking cookies. As you spend time together, the person will be able to practice speaking English. This will be fun for both of you.

Ask for an adult's help. Look at the books on your shelf at home. Are there books that your family has outgrown—or no longer needs? Donate these books to a group who is teaching English as a Second Language or to a recreation center. Ask the group or center what other needs that they have. Talk with your parents or a group at church about what you learned.

Loving Like Jesus

I don't like to boast. All parents are proud of their children and I'm no exception—I am a father who is proud of his sons.

Andrew, my eldest is a fine man. He is always faithful. When a job needs to be done, I know that I can count on Andrew. Andrew learned the family business well. He began taking responsibility at an early age. I came to depend on Andrew for help with the business. I don't know what I would have done without Andrew during the last period of cold weather. He was diligent in managing every detail of the business and saved us much money. Andrew is shrewd in dealing with other business people, too.

Benjamin, my youngest, came into the family business over recent years. Benjamin has always been a creative person. He liked the family business, but he took a little longer to learn his job. Benjamin likes to be with people. Benjamin is good with the employees. He likes to get to know people. Benjamin remembers the employee's birthdays and knows when an employee's family has a new baby. I don't mean that Benjamin doesn't do his job, but he likes people too.

In their free time, both of my sons enjoyed their friends. I was proud to see that my children were popular. They both played on sports teams in the community. Both Andrew and Benjamin were members of various community clubs. But Benjamin was very popular with his friends. He seemed to spend more time partying than taking care of his responsibilities with the family business. I must tell you that I was worried about Benjamin.

Finally, one day I decided to talk to Benjamin. But before I could find a time to talk to him, Benjamin came to me. He asked for his inheritance—his share of the family business now. He didn't want to wait until I died to receive his part of my wealth. I was surprised. I know that I am getting older. I won't live forever and all that I have is for my children. As is Jewish custom, Andrew as the eldest receives two-thirds of the business and Benjamin receives one-third. So we decided on an amount of money, and I gave Benjamin his part of the business.

Benjamin left home the next day. I felt like he had become friends with the 'wrong crowd.' I wasn't sure where he went. I didn't hear from him for a long time. Then one of my employees thought they saw him working in a Gentile country. I missed my son so much.

Not too long ago, I was sitting out on the front porch of my home. As I was looking at the beautiful sunset, I saw someone coming up the road. Do you know who it was? It was Benjamin! My son had come home.

I was so thankful for Benjamin's safety, I ran out to meet him. Poor Benjamin. He was skin and bones. He looked like it had been days since he ate a full meal. His clothes were torn and dirty. He had not had a bath for a long time. And Benjamin had no shoes to protect his feet.

When I met him on the road, Benjamin began to tell me how sorry he was for sinning against me and heaven. Benjamin then asked to return as an employee. He even offered to work outside. I stopped Benjamin from talking. I called for an employee to bring a new change of clothes, some new shoes, and a ring for his finger. I ordered another to start preparing a feast. Benjamin and all the family would eat well tonight.

At that moment I was very happy. When Benjamin first left home, it was as if he was dead. Yet when he came home, it was as if he was living again. But Andrew didn't see the situation that way. When he came home from work, the party had already started. Andrew would not come to the party, so I went to talk to him.

Andrew was angry. When I talked to him, Andrew reminded me that he was a good son. Andrew had obeyed me all of his life and I had never given a party for him and his friends. Andrew reminded me that his brother had been in a foreign country and wasted all of his money. Andrew accused me of being unfair.

All I could respond to Andrew was that I loved him, too. Andrew was always with me and all that I own would be his one day. I asked Andrew to be happy with me. His brother was lost and had been found.

I forgive Benjamin for leaving, but Andrew is my son, too. I love both my sons. I will always forgive when they sin against me.

(based on Luke 15:11–32)

What Does This Mean to Me?

Think about the answers to these questions and write them below.

Is there someone who likes you enough to call you by name?   Yes   No

If yes, who calls you by name? _____

_____

How do you feel when you are called by your name?

_____

_____

Think of a time when you and a parent or grandparent or adult friend did something together. Did you feel special?   Yes   No

Have you ever done something that this special person didn't like?
                    Yes   No

Did this person forgive you?   Yes   No

   Sin separates us from God just like you might have felt separated from this special person when you did something he or she did not like. We all sin. But just like the father in the story, God loves us and does not want to be separated from you. If you confess—tell God about your sin—and ask God to forgive you, God will always forgive you. God does not want to be separated from you. That is a promise from God. God loves every person.

JOURNAL

In your journal, describe yourself and how you are different from any other person. Write a prayer of thanksgiving for your unique qualities. If you need to at this time, confess to God anything that separates you from God. Thank God for God's forgiveness.

It's Up to Me

Choose one friend who does not come to church, or does not come to church very often. Pray for this person—but don't tell them you are praying for them. Ask God to help this person know that they are special to you and to God. Invite this person to a church activity with you. Introduce this person to others at church.

Ask your family or your pastor at church for the name of a person who lives alone. Bake chocolate chip cookies or put together a basket of fruit for this person. Arrange to visit this person to tell them how special they are to you and to God. At holidays include this person in your family plans—be sure to ask your parents first.

Forgiveness Times

Use a separate piece of paper to create your own forgiveness newspaper. Interview people at church about times they felt forgiven by a person or by God. Use these interviews to create your newspaper.

Choices

"Priest-Approved Sacrifices" "Pure Birds and Animals" "Change Your Change Here" "Best Prices in the Temple" "Sacrifices for Less" "Temple Souvenirs—Take some home to the family" "Clean Rooms for Rent"

Ah, the sweet sound of commerce heard inside and outside the Temple. Everyone in the Holy City knows that a festival is coming. It seems that everyone in Jerusalem is trying to make money. During holy seasons, vendors can sell things to the visitors in the city.

Hi, I'm Julius. I've been changing money in the Temple for over ten years now. In the beginning, I was one of two or three people who had special permission to set up a table and exchange the foreign money into sanctuary half shekels. People came with Greek, Roman, Syrian, and Egyptian coins. We charged our modest fee change to temple shekels. In the early days no one complained about our small fees. We were performing a service for all the Jewish men who came to the Temple to worship.

Today, dozens of money changers fill both the outside and the inside of the Temple. And now, farmers come into the city bringing their smelly animals to sell for sacrifices. Temple inspectors allow some of these animals to be holy sacrifices. But often the animals are rejected. Merchants inside the Temple charge very high prices for animals approved for sacrifice. The travelers who come to the Temple probably could not afford to buy two animals for sacrifice, but what else could they do?

This morning started out like any other day during Passover. Many of the Gentiles came to the outer area of the Temple to pray. Pilgrims arrived from other towns. People lined up for their turn with the Temple inspectors. Animals for sacrifice were bleating as they were dragged to the inner Temple. I was busy at my money exchange booth. I guess I have an honest face.

I did notice a small group of men coming into the Temple. They seemed to want to stay together around this one man. I assumed that this man was a leader. The leader seemed to be looking all around the Temple watching every person. I completed my exchange and watched this leader. I think I heard someone call Him Jesus.

In a few moments Jesus went over to one of the tables where animals were for sale. On the table there were cords used to tie animals. Jesus picked up a handful of the cords and tied them together.

Jesus' face was red and I could tell that He was angry. He used the cords to drive the animals out of the Temple. People around scattered like leaves in the wind. Jesus turned tables over, spilling the money on the marble floor of the Temple. The animals ran for cover.

I had a small table, so I picked it up and ran for the door. As I ran, I looked back to see Jesus at the booth where birds were for sale.

"Get these birds out of here! Take away the animals and the money tables! The house of God shall be called a house of prayer, but you have made it a place of robbers!" He shouted.

I don't know much of what happened after I left the Temple that day. I heard that the Jewish leaders of the Temple had many questions for Jesus. The leaders did not like Jesus interfering with the business at the Temple. The Jewish leaders even tried to find a way to kill Jesus. But the leaders saw that Jesus was very popular with the people.

Jesus did return to the Temple over the next few days. I went back myself a couple of times. Jesus taught for hours. Many people came to listen to Him.

I had forgotten what the Temple was about. It is a place to come and worship God. Jesus changed my life that day. I was never the same again.

(based on Luke 19:45-46)

What Does This Mean to Me?

Think about the answers to these questions and statements, then write them below.

What are some choices that you make at home? at school? at church? with friends? _____

_____

_____

_____

_____

_____

In your list above, put an "X" beside the choices that are hard to make.

Do you ask for help in making these hard choices?
yes   no

Whom do you ask for help in making these hard

choices? _____

For one week, write in your journal about your choices. Write about who helped you make the choices. Were the choices good choices or poor choices? At the end of each journal entry, write a short prayer asking God to help you make the best choices.

It's Up to Me

Adopt a grandparent at a nursing home. Ask an adult to help you contact the activities director or another nursing home administrator. You may ask the director to tell you about a senior adult who has few visitors or one who needs a friend. Visit this person as often as you can. Tell the grandparent about your family, your school, and your church. Think of ways to spend time with your adopted grandparent. Pray for your adopted grandparent.

Ask some friends to help you present a musical program or play for some persons at a nursing home or retirement center. Ask an adult to help you contact the nursing home to set up a time for your musical program or play. This might be done around a holiday time.

If your church records your worship services for people who cannot attend, ask for ways that you can help that ministry.

Keep Learning from Jesus

I've learned so much from our life with Jesus. When I left my home to follow Jesus, I didn't realize how my life would change.

I've watched Jesus change water into wine at a wedding. We as disciples have seen Jesus feed thousands from one little boy's lunch. People with leprosy and crippled men have been healed because of Jesus' touch.

Jesus has tried to teach us to trust by calming stormy waters. We sometimes understand Jesus' lessons, but sometimes we don't understand.

We were sent out to other towns to care for people and to heal people. Some of us returned with good reports, but some of us were not so successful. Jesus keeps on trying to teach us.

We had heard Jesus pray all during our time together. Jesus would often go away into a quiet place to pray. Sometimes I would wake up at night and hear Jesus praying. Jesus' prayers were always beautiful. When Jesus prayed, you could tell He was praying to God.

Recently, one of the disciples asked Jesus, "Lord, teach us to pray, just as John taught his followers to pray."

I don't know why we hadn't thought to ask Jesus

this question before now. Rabbis were known to teach their students prayers. These prayers could be used daily. But, here's what Jesus taught us to answer our question;
"Father, may your holy name be honored;
may your kingdom come.
Give us day by day the food we need.
Forgive us our sins,
for we forgive everyone who does us wrong.
And do not bring us to hard testing" (Luke 11:2–4 CEV).

The prayer is really a simple one. Here's what I learned from our lesson from Jesus that day.

We are to begin the prayer by calling God Father. When we pray we are not talking to someone who doesn't know us. We are praying to our God who loves us and cares for us like a loving, caring parent. We can talk to God just like we talk to someone who loves us and cares for us. We can talk to God like a friend.

May your holy name be honored tells us that we are still learning more and more about God. For us as Jewish men, our name is not only what our friends call us when they talk to us. Our name is who we are. This part of the prayer means we know who God is and we trust God.

The next words, may your kingdom come, are more words of respect for God. We as pray-ers are remembering that God is God. God is more than we as human beings are. God knows all things. God knows about the earth and our lives better than we know. We are asking for God's perfect timing, place, and actions to come into our lives. We are putting God first before ourselves.

The next part of the prayer are the personal requests prayed to God. In the prayer we ask God for three things. The first request is give us day by day the food we need. We are asking God to give us the food, drink, clothing, rest, energy, and knowledge that we need for our day to live.

We also ask God to forgive us our sins for we forgive everyone who has done us wrong. We are praying to ask God to forgive us because we have done things wrong in our past.

Thirdly we ask God, do not bring us to hard testing. We know that every day we must make choices. We are asking God to help us make good choices.

Jesus taught us to pray this way. We disciples still use this prayer. Since Jesus needed to pray, I know that I need to also.

(based on Luke 11: 1-4)

What Does This Mean to Me?

Think about the answers to these questions, then write them below.

What is prayer to you?

_____

_____

_____

_____

_____

Do you pray?   yes   no

If you answered yes, why do you pray?

_____
_____
_____
_____
_____

What do you pray about?

_____
_____
_____
_____

When do you pray?

_____
_____
_____
_____

Use your questions and answers above. Interview three adults about prayer. Ask the adults the same questions. Share with them what you are learning about prayer. You may want to interview at least one person who is not a part of your church.

JOURNAL

Write in your journal what you learned from the interviews on the previous page.
Did you learn something new about prayer?

It's Up to Me

Invite a friend or a family member to be your prayer partner. Talk together about prayer. Plan a time to pray together once a week. Pray for personal needs, and pray for people who don't know Jesus.

Ask a parent and a leader at church to set up a Sock Tree. Set a large branch in a stand. Invite people at church to bring socks to hang on the tree. When the tree is full, give the socks to a homeless shelter or a clothing closet.

Write a letter to a college student who is away from home. Ask your pastor or another leader at church for a student's name and address. In the letter tell the student about yourself and share what you are learning about prayer. Pray for the student.

Begin a Prayer List

Your prayer list may be a bookmark or an index card that you list people or things that you pray for each day. You may want to pray for your family on one day, your friends on one day, your school activities on another day and your church leaders on another day.

Sunday	Monday	Tuesday	Wednesday
Thursday	Friday	Saturday	Every Day

Caring for the Person

On a beautiful warm Sabbath morning, the swish of a woman's robe and the slap, slap, slap of the leather sandals can be heard coming up the synagogue steps. Abby is coming to worship and pray.

"Welcome Abby. Good to see you today," and "Blessings Abby. Glad you came to worship today," are the greetings that Abby hears as she enters the synagogue.

Abby responds cheerfully, "Blessings to you both. It's wonderful to hear your voice."

Abby has been crippled for eighteen years. She is completely bent over and cannot stand up straight. Some people say that her crooked back was caused by an evil spirit. Pain is a part of Abby's daily life. Walking is probably very difficult for Abby, but she comes to the synagogue every week.

People in town know Abby, but the synagogue leaders do not pay her much attention. She does not bring a large offering to synagogue. She loves people, but she cannot do things for others. She is a small, bent-over woman.

On this Sabbath day, Jesus is teaching at Abby's synagogue. Jesus looks over His students and sees Abby. Jesus sees Abby's patience, love, and crippled body.

Jesus calls Abby over to Him." Woman, you are free from your sickness," He says to her. Jesus places His hands on Abby's body and a miracle happens. Abby stands up straight. She looks Jesus in the eyes.

Everyone at synagogue that day sees the joy on Abby's face. Abby immediately praises God.

After this happens, all the people around Abby praise God. Abby's friends offer prayers of thanksgiving for Abby's healing. Truly, it is good to be in the house of the Lord on this day.

But there are some synagogue leaders who are angry. The synagogue leaders do not like Jesus. They are looking for a way to criticize Jesus.

"There are six days to work in a week. This woman should have come to be healed on one of those days," the synagogue president states loudly. The synagogue president tells Jesus that healing is work. Good Jewish people do not work on the Sabbath. He thinks he will make Jesus look foolish.

But Jesus responds, "Are you trying to fool someone? We all will untie a donkey and take it for water on the Sabbath. Why should I not care for a human being as well as you care for an animal on the Sabbath?"

Now the synagogue leaders look foolish. They are embarrassed by their thoughts and words.

All the other people at synagogue this day— and Abby—are rejoicing. They sing songs of praise and thanksgiving to God. Abby sits tall on the synagogue bench. Abby has come to the synagogue to praise God.

Jesus has come to synagogue this day, knowing that each person is important. Rules are important, but people are more important than rules.

(based on Luke 13:10-17)

What Does This Mean to Me?

Think about the answers to these questions, then write them below.

Look around at school or at church. Is there someone who is new or doesn't dress like everyone else, or usually sits alone, or someone who has trouble walk-ing, or someone who doesn't act friendly? Write that person's name here.

_____

Is this person important to your group?
      yes   no

Is this person important to God?
      yes   no

What are two ways that you might be a friend to this person? _____
_____
_____
_____
_____
_____
_____

JOURNAL

Pretend that you are Abby from our story. In your journal, write about her life before Jesus healed her. Then write a prayer of thanksgiving to God.

It's Up to Me

Make fold-over note cards for a hospital chaplain or your pastor as they visit persons who are sick. Use construction paper or a paper that is thicker than notebook paper. Cut the paper in half. Fold the half-sheets in half. Use thin markers or crayons to decorate the front of the card. Include a scripture verse on the card. You might use:

 "Let us love one another, because love comes from God" (1 John 4:7a CEV).

"The Lord is my rock, my fortress, and my deliverer; my God is my rock, in whom I take refuge" (Psalms 18:2a NIV).

"I will praise you, Lord, with all my heart" (Psalms 9:1a CEV).

Gather paper or plastic grocery bags from family, friends, or neighbors. Donate these bags to a food bank or church food pantry in your town. Ask the food bank or food pantry for other ways that you can help.